GET PUBLISHED
NAVIGATE THE
PUBLISHING PROCESS
WITH CONFIDENCE

VICTOR KWEGYIR

THE CONFIDENT AUTHOR SERIES:
MASTER THE ART OF WRITING, PUBLISHING, AND STRATEGICALLY
PROMOTING YOUR BOOK FOR SUCCESS

GET PUBLISHED
Navigate The Publishing Process With Confidence

Copyright © 2025 by Victor Kwegyir
All rights reserved.

Unless otherwise indicated, all quotes are taken
from *Business 365: Daily Inspiration for Creativity, Innovation and Business Success* by Victor Kwegyir [1]

Publisher
Vike Springs Publishing Ltd.
www.vikesprings.com

First Edition
ISBN-13: 978-1-0686219-9-4- E-book
ISBN-13: 978-1-918185-00-3- Paperback
ISBN-13: 978-1-918185-01-0- Audiobook

Printed in the United Kingdom and United States of America

For bulk orders, book writing, coaching and publishing services, as well as bookings for speaking engagements, contact us:
admin@vikesprings.com

TITLE:	Get Published: Navigate the Publishing Process with Confidence
AUTHOR:	Victor Kwegyir
PUBLISH DATE:	1st November
Imprint:	Vike Springs Publishing Ltd

GET PUBLISHED is your step-by-step guide to navigating the publishing world with clarity and confidence—covering everything from editing and design to pricing, formats, and choosing the right publishing path.

Key Talking Points

1. **Demystifies Publishing Options** – Clear guidance on traditional, self, and hybrid publishing, helping authors choose the best route for their goals.

2. **Covers Every Stage of Production** – From editing, layout, and proofreading to cover design, blurbs, bios, ISBNs, and pricing strategies—nothing is left out.

3. **Avoids Costly Mistakes** – Insider advice from an experienced publisher ensures your book is produced professionally and positioned for success in print, eBook, and audio formats.

Contact name:	Victor Kwegyir
Email:	admin@vikesprings.com

LIMIT OF LIABILITY/DISCLAIMER OF WARRANTY

DEDICATION

To those who value the publishing world – whether hard print, electronic format, or audio –
I would like to thank you for recognising the hard work of bringing a book to print and buying the books we produce.

I also dedicate this book to those who spread the word to others when they read, and who appreciate the work written by our authors.

The team at Vike Springs continues to build a strong reputation of producing quality books for you, and I hope you will continue to support our work.

CONTENTS

INTRODUCTION

Welcome to the world of publishing. Salman Rushdie, in *Joseph Anton: A Memoir*, says "When a book leaves its author's desk it changes. Even before anyone has read it, before eyes other than its creator's have looked upon a single phrase, it is irretrievably altered. It has become *a book that can be read*, that no longer belongs to its maker. It has acquired, in a sense, free will. It will make its journey through the world and there is no longer anything the author can do about it. Even he, as he looks at its sentences, reads them differently now that they can be read by others. They look like different sentences. The book has gone out into the world and the world has remade it."[2]

Whatever stage your book is at, you will reach the point where it is ready to go out into the world, and that involves publishing. Many first-time authors believe that all that needs to happen after they have 'finished' their book is a simple production process. However, you will soon discover through reading *Get Published* that much more is involved: navigating the publishing process involves preparation, research and resilience.

Your newly written book will mean a lot to you for various reasons. It may be a passion, the realisation of a dream, the beginning of a new career path, or a way you are going to establish your expertise and build a legacy. You may wish to be consulted as an authority on a subject, to be part of a lecture circuit or develop a training programme; or you may want to expand your scope of influence as you share your vision or concerns. You may also want to have a secure source of financial income. Or it may be a combination, or all, of the above.

What many people fail to understand is that the publishing process is interlinked, and each stage impacts the final goal. To get the best results you must give attention to each stage to ensure that it's delivered professionally. Many start the process with little consideration for quality outcomes, but rather only think about how cheaply they can publish their book. There are many companies that take advantage of aspiring authors, promising much but delivering little, largely because even though the publishing process has been significantly simplified over the last couple of decades, to get it right there are a number of steps and processes that need to be managed well.

You will realise that this process involves editing, designing, formatting, proofreading, distributing and printing. I explain the differences between hardcover, paperback, electronic eBook formatting, and audiobooks, and you will be encouraged to take into account the way your publication can be marketed, so that your book doesn't languish in no-man's land, where few sales are realised. Instead it will be sold, read and become a great success.

As you begin to know more about the different aspects of publishing, this understanding will help you to decide how you want to proceed. You may be one of many who have tried and failed to get your writing published, whether through your own circumstances, or by being let down via the publication route you tried. Please don't give up, but take a look at your situation again, and find a way forward. It may be that you need to revisit how you are presenting your writing – to know more about who you want your reader to be, reassess your publishing goal, and understand more about how to convey your unique angle and style. You may also need to re-assess your route to market – your pricing, retail targeting, strategy for distribution, and the way you will promote your book, and yourself. Whatever areas you need to reassess, be assured that there is professional help available to assist you to reach your goal to become a successful published author.

This is the second book in *The Confident Author Series: Master the Art of Writing, Publishing, and Strategically Promoting Your Book for Success*. These books are not meant to be digested in a linear fashion – even when starting your writing journey, you will need to be aware of the next steps, what you require as far as publication options, and how you can market your product. Throughout this series of books you will find quotes from one of my other books, *Business 365: Daily Inspiration for Creativity, Innovation and Business Success* to encourage and motivate as you move towards becoming a published author.

"You do not grow and become successful by default.
You have to learn and take sound advice along the way."

CHAPTER
1

WHAT IS PUBLISHING?

To publish means to make information and literature available for the public to view. Publishing involves the process of producing and distributing literature so that the public can have access to it.

The original meaning of the word 'publishing' was to print newspapers and books on paper and then distribute them. This began with the invention and use of the printing press in the 1500s. Traditionally, publishing houses would buy the copyright to an author's work, and then would print, distribute and sell it. Royalties – generally a percentage of overall sales – would be earned by the author.

TRADITIONAL PUBLISHING

Traditional publishers, or trad publishers, are predisposed towards well-known names or authors who already have published books, and who will attract an audience. They need to be confident on a return on their investment. This is a highly competitive arena where you will need a publishing agent to direct your submission to potential publishing companies, many of whom have specific submission guidelines. A sound literary agent will not charge an upfront fee for any services they provide, and commission should not be charged if they do not secure a publisher for your book.

An advantage of using trad publishers is their established distribution and sales infrastructure, but be advised that it is difficult to get an opening in this area and you may still need to be heavily involved in marketing.

SELF-PUBLISHING

Self-publishing is booming nowadays. The author acts as the publisher, and they get to keep all the income from their sales and retain copyright (for both contents and publishing). They can determine all aspects of how they place their books in the market and how they choose to sell. They are solely responsible for publishing their paper copy books or uploading them electronically. ISBNs are purchased and assigned in their own publishing name as the publisher. Someone who is self-publishing totally independently of any publishing support, however, will have to invest a considerable amount of time in editing, design and marketing, and it is wise to recognise that the effort may involve falling down one of the many pitfalls along the way.

Sometimes called 'Assisted Self-Publishing', or 'Vanity Publishing', this has suffered from a bad press in the past, due to low standards and high fees by some providers. Nowadays many people who use assisted self-publishing companies find they are proving to be high quality and professional, with a 'gold standard' reputation for bringing books to market in a way that rivals the trad publishing route. They deliver quality editing, design and print services adhering to industry standards, and provide established links to promote, market and distribute their books. They offer reliable advice on every stage of your writing journey, so that you are aware of all the elements of getting your book to your readership. There is an upfront cost, of course, but the advantage of this route is that you get to keep all the proceeds from your sales.

Vike Springs offers self-publishing services by taking on all the hassle of the publishing process on behalf of the author. They advise and facilitate the entire publishing process on behalf of the self-publisher. In this case Vike Springs Publishing is NOT the publisher, but through our comprehensive packages we facilitate the entire process (writing, editing, proofreading, formatting, printing, distribution on all platforms, etc.) and once the book is published we can hand over all the accounts to the author to manage, or we manage it on their behalf.

HYBRID PUBLISHING

Hybrid publishing is another aspect of self-publishing. This is where a publishing house will provide a variety of services for you for an up-front fee. They contribute their expertise, and you in return get to keep all your income from sales and retain copyright. The fee you pay will depend on the range of services you decide upon.

Independent or hybrid publishers will facilitate the publishing process for anyone, whatever their reason for writing a book. They can deliver excellent quality in editing and publishing services, and will advise on your marketing strategy.

When an author signs up to any of Vike Springs hybrid publishing packages, a contractual relationship is established whereby Vike Springs Publishing becomes the legal publisher and owns the publishing rights. The author owns the copyright of the contents. A contractual agreement between publisher and author with the details is discussed, agreed on and signed, before commencement of the project.

"The amount of resources you are willing to spend on preparation and planning says everything about how much faith you have in your dream!"

OTHER TYPES OF HYBRID PUBLISHING

Partnership Publishing

This is a collaborative arrangement where the author retains creative control, but shares financial risks with the publisher, who is responsible for production and marketing. As an author, you do not get an advance, and you do not keep all of the profits from your sales. This co-publishing arrangement means you and your publisher are both invested in getting good outcomes, and it is becoming a popular option for authors who want to continue to have a say in what happens to their books.

Crowdfunded Publishing

With this approach, the author campaigns to raise funds to publish the book. When sufficient funds have been established, publication will proceed and the investors will receive copies of the publication. Writers can ask for their readers' support, securing funds for their projects while building an audience. With crowdfunding you turn passionate readers into investors and advocates.[3]

> *"In life, in business and in your career, someone or something has to introduce you to your next level of promotion, platform or breakthrough. The question is, what will they/it say about you and your abilities."*

SOME FACTS AND FIGURES ABOUT PUBLISHING

According to one survey conducted globally, among authors who published their first book in the last 10 years, more self-published authors (1,600) have earned over $25,000 a year than traditionally published authors (1,200). [4]

Self-publishing has created an entirely new ecosystem of services, i.e. cover design, marketing, and distribution. The result is an influx of industry professionals who offer specialised services to self-published authors. It has levelled the playing field and allowed these authors to compete head-to-head with traditionally published content. [5]

For the years 2025 to 2035, the UK publishing market is expected to grow at a Compound Annual Growth Rate (CAGR) of 3.6%, and 3.8% in the US. [6]

Self-published authors made up over 50% of Kindle's Top 400 Books for 2023[7]. This is a remarkable figure and serves to illustrate how the trad publishing route is being overtaken by self- and hybrid-publishing.

In recent years, the audiobook industry has experienced an era of remarkable growth as well, with audiobook publishers reporting double-digit growth in revenue over the past ten years. According to Wordsrated, a research organisation conducting data-driven analysis on the publishing industry, the audiobook industry will continue to grow, and is expected to be worth about $35.05 billion in 2030.[8]

GW & Co. reports that in 2023, the audiobook segment of book publishing generated a remarkable $5.4 billion, with the USA alone contributing $1.8 billion.[9]

By 2025 to 2035, the market is set to experience transformative growth as AI-assisted editing, personalised content recommendations, and immersive storytelling experiences all become mainstream.[10]

"Success can come in different forms and levels, but the principles behind it are one and the same."

CHAPTER

2

THE FIRST STEP – DEVELOPMENT AND ACQUISITION

The development and acquisition stage is the first step in your journey from completed manuscript to published book. The term originates with trad publishing but it is still used today as the initial stage in engaging a hybrid publisher, where the author is arranging and paying for a range of services to get their book published.

In trad publishing, the acquisition part is where the publisher acquires the rights to the book in a negotiated deal through a literary agent, who has agreed to represent you. The deal may involve an advance, and at this stage a percentage of the royalties from the sale of the published book is agreed.

The development aspect of this stage is the process where the publisher's editor works collaboratively with the author to make changes to the book in order to make it marketable and ready for publication. This may involve rewriting and revising, and may also involve bringing the book into the recognised 'house style' – a system to standardise spelling, layout, punctuation and phraseology. The author does not retain creative control of the book, as it becomes subject to the requirements of the publisher.

With self- and hybrid publishing, the author will decide on the range of services they want to make use of, which may be influenced by the amount they want to pay. For example, they may want to use the editing stage and formatting (layout and design) stage, and then proceed to proofread and print themselves, and manage their own promotion and marketing, or they may want the whole package. Once they agree the 'package', then the process will begin in order to develop the book so it is ready for print.

A note about timescales here. Trad publishing is a slow process, taking up to two years before a book is ready for release. This timescale does not take into account the search for a literary agent who will take on your book and submit it to the publishing house – that in itself can take a long time. Self-publishing is far quicker – it can be almost instant and your book will be rapidly uploaded onto various self-publishing outlets. Hybrid publishing is significantly faster than trad publishing, and will depend on the range of services you choose. However, the turnaround time will vary depending on the publishing company you use, so it is wise to check the timings of the processes you agree to before you sign.

Let me state here that some self-publishing services such as Vike Springs Publishing work on the principle that they do not reject any manuscript but commit to work with the author to perfect the manuscript to the highest standard and quality.

Another consideration is the degree of control you will have over your writing. As you might imagine, trad publishers will exert more control over your book, and you may think that hybrid publishers will agree with your preferences. However, some hybrid publishers will want to ensure that your book meets their publishing standards and fits in with their 'stable' of other publications.

Whatever route you choose, make sure you understand all aspects of the contract you agree to. These include aspects of copyright, timelines, and distribution agreements.

> *"Keep your focus, don't be distracted by what everyone else is doing. Be persistent and consistent, with a good strategy."*

CHAPTER

3

FURTHER STEPS IN PUBLISHING

The following headings describe the various aspects of the publishing process. You will probably not need to know all the details of every stage, but it will help to have a broad understanding of what your professional publishing team will be providing to perfect your book for its launch.

Of course, many people these days opt to do the work of publisher themselves. Some dispense with editors and proofreaders, others attempt the work of layout, cover design and production. You can see the results of poor amateur work quite clearly, and this often reflects in sales and reviews.

WRITING

Covered in our first book, *Get Writing*, ghostwriting is an option for those who have the ideas but don't feel they have the time, the skillset, or the self-discipline needed in order to write books themselves. Another option is a step away from a ghostwriter providing all the text, and that is when a writer co-writes, or re-writes, your content. This is termed developmental writing. When others write for you in these situations, the writer does not receive any credit or recognition, and you are named as the author, retaining the rights of copy, or copyright.

BLURBS (BOOK DESCRIPTIONS) AND AUTHOR BIO

Your book will need to have a written blurb that will appear on the back cover, or in the description of your eBook. This is an art form in itself, as a well-written blurb will sell your book by inviting the prospective buyer to invest in it. Avoid clichés, aim to grab your reader's attention and tease them into wanting to discover more. Blurbs average between 100 and 200 words, though there are exceptions to this, and your book description will sometimes depend on how much space you have on your book cover.

The author bio is written in the third person, is about 200 words in length, and introduces the author to readers, publishers, and booksellers. Your author bio will convey your credibility as an authority on the subject you are writing about and may describe your journey or your reasons for writing your book. Author bios are also used in promotional materials. They build a relationship with your audience.

Blurbs and author bios should contain key words that feed into your metadata and help sell your book. This is covered further in book three of this series: *Promote Your Book.*

EDITING, PROOFREADING AND OTHER WAYS TO CHECK YOUR MANUSCRIPT

Editing and proofreading are essential to ensure your book is error free. A book that has been expertly edited and proofread conveys a message to the reader that the author has a professional approach to their work and is reliable. It leads readers to believe in the book, and avoids them being distracted by errors and mistakes. Typically editors will go through the manuscript a number of times, looking at the detail in different ways, to make sure they pick up all the gremlins. They will submit their work to the author with the changes they have made clearly highlighted.

A Word About Style Sheets

Style sheets are often used by companies or publishers to set out the rules for writing. Style sheets are also used by authors to explain terms used, characteristics of the people in the story, and any anomalies. Style sheets are also useful when working with a series of books, where knowledge is needed of how things were previously set out. Having a style sheet means everyone involved in the production of the book has a way to check any queries they have, and it avoids changes being made that have already been dealt with.

TYPES OF EDITING

You may be surprised to learn that there are different forms of editing, and that editing is distinctly different from proofreading.

Developmental editing looks for consistency in the plot, development of characters, and a logical flow of the story. It considers the big picture. A developmental editor will suggest changes in structure, adding or repositioning chapters. There will also be improvements required in language and detail. Authors may be guided to be clearer with planning and developing the outline and structure, and inconsistencies with the plot will be identified. If there is a lot of dialogue, information may be given so that this becomes more vibrant and genuine. Developmental editors may suggest more character development or depth of information.

Line editing improves the flow of the text, focusing on sentence structure and style. It takes out detail that is not necessary to the story. A line editor will focus on tone and style, and seek to clarify what the author intends to communicate, pointing out inconsistencies. There may be an inconsistency with data being presented (non-fiction) or a character's description (fiction), or information may be fact checked and shown to be incorrect. Sentence structure may be changed to bring clarity or rhythm and paragraphs may be shortened if too long, or combined if too short.

Copyediting focuses on punctuation, grammar, spelling and consistency. Headings and lists will be set out clearly, and capitalisation of certain words will be standardised. A copyeditor will ensure that the way numbers are shown are consistent, and that language is for example, in UK or US English throughout. There may be overuse of a particular phrase or word that could be changed to improve the narrative. There are many aspects to a copyeditor's role, and these will vary depending on the type of book they are working on.

There is generally overlap with these different editing roles. Some authors will feel confident enough in their writing to just have a copyeditor review the work, others will need the assistance of all three through the stages of editing and re-writing.

USING A BETA READER

A beta reader is someone who reads your book before publication in order to give feedback. The term 'beta' originated in the software industry, where new versions were tested before release. Beta readers will highlight issues with the plot or with the pacing. They will assess if the book will meet the outcomes that the author is aiming for.

Beta readers can be found from a fan base, or industry professionals, such as writers or editors.

If you choose to use a beta reader to get feedback on your writing, be clear about what you expect or need from them, and be open to receiving constructive criticism.

PROOFREADING

Proofreading is the actual process of reading through the proof before print. It is generally the final part of the checking process, after the work has been converted from a word processing document, generally Word, to a PDF. In this final check the proofreader is not there to suggest changes to what you have written, but only to make sure that it is correct from a grammatical point of view, that the punctuation is accurate, that there is consistency, that all headings are correctly laid out, and that there are no typographical or formatting errors in the layout of the book. A proofreader will also check that page breaks are set out correctly and that any footnotes, references, and list of contents are laid out in the right way.

When authors and editors have used a style sheet, proofreaders will use the rules that have been listed to double-check accuracy.

SECOND THOUGHTS

How do you know when your manuscript is complete? Many authors have a crisis of confidence at this stage of publication. This loss of confidence can mean they never actually send the manuscript to the publishers because they believe it can be improved, and each time they review what they have written they find themselves adding more to the contents. It is estimated that up to 97% of writers never finish or submit their manuscript for publishing.

You also have authors who submit the work for editing and even have it set out by the designer so it's ready to go, but the thought of actually going into print is overwhelming, and so they step back, and begin to think of how they can improve their manuscript and add more changes. As you can imagine, doing this disrupts the process or robs you of ever getting the process underway where you can benefit from the immense help professional editors can offer. It also puts you at risk of ever getting the book published at all. When many changes are made at this stage of the process, it can expose the book to more errors that may not be spotted before the print run, and that can be costly.

The way to avoid this common pitfall is to make sure you use the editing team at the editing stage and trust their professionalism. Try to identify any queries you have or any ideas about changes as early as you can, and certainly before the editing work has been completed and is agreed. You can be reassured that our professional editors will listen to your concerns and address any issues you may have, including any amendments at the appropriate stage of the process. So many people fail to recognise the value of good editing, and the support and confidence that writers can gain, especially at this point.

Learn to trust the inspiration you had as you began to write, and the strong original vision of what you wanted to say. Affirm that initial spark that has enabled you to get to the point of finishing your book and approaching the reality of seeing it in print.

Tell yourself that when you say 'go' so that your manuscript can go to design and layout, you have crafted the work as best as you can, your editing team can be trusted, and any thoughts you may have about how you could have done things differently are good learning points for the future. In addition, any gaps or updates in your material can always be considered for a second edition of the book, or even another follow-up book on the subject.

IN SHORT

Editing and proofreading are essential steps to ensure your manuscript is polished and professional, and it is highly recommended that writers avail themselves of these checks. Investing in these stages will make sure you have a more compelling and error-free book, and will enhance your credibility as an author.

> *"The process is your friend and your best bet to achieve greater heights and success."*

CHAPTER
4

DESIGN

INTERIOR DESIGN AND FORMATTING YOUR BOOK

A great deal of work will go into the design and formatting of your book, whether it's for hardback and paperback printing, eBook, or the conversion to an audiobook.

Hardback and Paperback

The designer will establish the font size and headings, ensure consistent alignment, and set the correct margins to allow for binding. The print colour will also be adjusted for paper printing, referred to as CMYB (cyan, magenta, yellow and black). This colour format will also be used for any diagrams or pictures in your book, and the images must be high-resolution (300 dpi or higher) to avoid pixilation.

The final document will be saved into a print-ready format, commonly a PDF/X-1a file, and will initially be checked on screen, and then a proof will be printed where the colours, layout and format will be physically checked.

eBooks

You may think that this is a simple process, but if you have ever tried to read an eBook that has not been formatted correctly, you will know how important it is that it is done professionally. The overall requirement is that the eBook has ease of readability, whatever device is used.

There are a number of formatting tools such as Adobe InDesign, Scrivener, Vellum (Mac), Calibre (for conversion). The book will be formatted into EPUB for Amazon Kindle, Apple Books, Google Play Books, or Kobo. A PDF may also be used for fixed layout eBooks.

Some principles that should be followed are: a consistent heading style, short paragraphs, line spacing that's easy to read, and readable fonts with a larger font size for headings. Margins and the text should be aligned correctly. With eBooks it's advisable to avoid justified layout, as this will affect the spacing across the lines of text when the book is read on different devices. The colour also changes for screen reading, to RGB (red, green, blue).

All web links should be hyperlinked, so they can be accessed with a click, opening a new window. The list of contents should also be hyperlinked. Visuals such as images and tables need to be in the correct format.

Before it is released the eBook should be previewed and tested on various devices to ensure it is readable whatever the size of screen. Bear in mind that users can change orientation, typeface, font size and line spacing on their devices, which can affect the flow of text.

Widows and orphans. This is a term that is used to describe isolated lines of text at the beginning or end of a page. Because eBooks are fluid in the flow of text, as the text adjusts to different screen sizes and orientations, widow and orphan problems can be encountered if the book has not been formatted correctly. Other than the actual formatting, some ways to deal with this problem are to avoid using manual line breaks and use consistent paragraph styles. Short paragraphs will also help keep a paragraph within a page, and occasionally it may be necessary to adjust the content or wording to improve text flow.

Your design team will recommend publishing in PDF format where layout is critical, such as technical manuals, or books with complex formatting.

Audiobooks

As you might imagine, preparing an audiobook for release has its own peculiarities. The manuscript may have to be adapted by simplifying complex sentences, using tone and other verbal clues to describe what may be indicated visually. Depending on the nature of your book, you may decide to record an abridged version.

The choice of narrator should reflect the genre of the book, or if there are a lot of different characters there may be a need for multiple narrators. Audiobook recording should be done in a professional recording studio, or a soundproof environment, with the use of high quality recording equipment, and using audio editing software like Audacity, Adobe Audition or Pro Tools. The book will be recorded on different files, broken down by chapter.

The edited and final audiobook should have standardised volume levels and meet the industry standards for audio quality. The files will then be exported, usually to an MP3-enabled platform.

The audiobook should be 'prooflistened', and feedback from beta listeners will make sure the recording is error free.

There is a real skill in producing an audiobook so that it correctly reflects the pace and energy of the book in its written format.

"Attaining a different level of success without updating your knowledge base or changing environment is an uphill task."

COVER DESIGN

Your book title and your cover design are key elements of marketing your book, and there is a lot to consider. The design team will help you in this task, by making sure the cover appeals to your target audience, and stands out in a memorable way. Your designer will ensure that the cover conveys the genre, that the title is easy to read, and that your name is on the cover and easily identified. There are also important aspects involving the colour of the design and the clarity of the images that are used.

The design will be translated into eBook format, and will need to also apply to an audiobook if you are using that medium. So the publisher's requirements as to size of the covers will be taken into consideration.

Designing a cover also includes the back of the book, which will include a 'blurb' (description of the book), the author's bio, details of the publisher, and ISBN. The spine width for a hard copy or paperback book is also determined according to the number of pages of the book.

Designers will also ensure that any images used are properly licensed for use.

You may consider a number of design choices of book cover, seeking feedback as to which one has the most appeal and conveys what your book is about, before deciding on the final version. When choosing your cover, get feedback from your target reader group if you can, and make sure that your title and cover design reflect what is in your book. Think of it as an entry point – the doorway has to lead to what your reader hopes or expects to find.

The top tip for this aspect of publication is to aim to have the best book cover possible, whatever the cost, as a good cover is key to selling your book. Poor design will affect the appeal of your book and ultimately result in poor sales.

"Excellence opens doors and establishes you, whichever way you turn."

CHAPTER

5

PRINTING OPTIONS

By now you will have realised that getting a book to print has many facets.

Print options depend on budget and estimation of level of sales. Also consider your target audience: are they looking for value for money, or are they more likely to want to invest in a book that conveys sophistication and quality?

Many new authors opt for a print-on-demand service, as it removes the risk of ordering too many or too few copies at any given time, which involves the challenge of overstocking . It also offers the ability, if necessary, to update the contents easily and more cost-effectively along the way.

When choosing a print option, consider your budget, target audience, sales expectations, and the specific requirements of your book.

Print-on-demand offers flexibility and minimal risk for new and self-publishing authors.

Offset printing is cost-effective for large print runs and offers high quality.

Digital printing bridges the gap with good quality and cost-effectiveness for smaller runs.

Additionally, deciding between hardcover and paperback, as well as considering specialty options, will influence the overall presentation and market appeal of your book.

Your publisher will advise on the appropriate paper weight used for the book and for the cover, whether hardback or paperback, and the finish of the cover. There are four main binding methods depending on the nature of your book:

- saddle stitching, for booklets and magazines;
- perfect binding, often used for paperbacks;
- case binding, a traditional hardcover binding;
- spiral binding, used for manuals and workbooks.

Black and white printing is an acceptable choice for most publications, but the costlier colour option is necessary for books with graphics, illustrations, photographs, etc. The quantity and quality of colour required will also affect cost, which can be markedly higher than black and white, especially if printed in small runs.

When making decisions about print, you will need to balance quality with cost-effectiveness, together with your budget and projected sales.

Depending on the nature of your publication, there are many other specialisations involved, and your publisher can help you make informed decisions, and communicate with the printer on your behalf.

*"You can live your dreams if you remain focused on the treasure...
not the trouble."*

CHAPTER
6

CATEGORISING AND PRICING YOUR BOOK

ISBN AND UPC BARCODES

We are all familiar with ISBN codes, and UPC bar codes on products, but what do they really mean and how are they assigned?

The International Standard Book Number (ISBN) is a 13-digit number that identifies the edition, publication date and publisher. This is a global standard, so books can be identified worldwide.

ISBNs are issued by the ISBN Agency. A publisher registers with the national ISBN agency, which issues a unique prefix of three numbers which identifies where the publisher is based. Further numbers identify the publisher. The remaining numbers identify the publication title and format, e.g. paperback or eBook. There is also a further aspect of the ISBN that ensures the number is valid and unique. New ISBNs are assigned to new editions or formats of books, but not to general reprints. This numbering system simplifies ordering, inventory control, and managing sales, and its global aspect ensures that there is a clear way of identifying books internationally.

A Universal Product Code (UPC) is a scannable barcode used in retail for all sorts of products. It was developed originally for grocery checkouts, but then spread to other retail outlets. The reason this 12-digit numeric code is also found on printed material with ISBNs is that it gives any retailer the option to quickly scan for price at checkout and manage stock.

If you are making use of a hybrid publishing package, this is likely to include your ISBN assignment and UPC barcode. However, this is not always the case, and you may have to purchase it as an additional cost.

METADATA

Metadata is key to a good marketing and sales strategy. Metadata is described in more detail in the third of this series of books *Promote Your Book*, but in brief this is a way of describing your book so it can be easily found by the right reader, through searches, and be correctly categorised by librarians and booksellers.

QR CODES

In their basic form, QR codes appear alongside ISBN numbers and UPC barcodes. They provide a way for people to access all formats of the book they are interested in, and get instant access to a purchase point.

As the name implies, static QR codes are codes where the information is entered at the generation of the box code, whereas dynamic QR codes can be updated with all sorts of current information that may be useful to the prospective purchaser, including latest reviews, special offers, news of other publications etc.

QR codes are also covered in *Promote Your Book* as a vital tool to aid marketing, because not only can they convey basic information about your book, but also provide links to further information, such as video links or links to social media.

PRICE

Your publisher will advise on pricing, but it is useful to keep the following details in mind, to ensure that your book is priced at a competitive rate but is also profitable. Pricing will be different for eBooks, paperback, hardback and audiobooks.

Research price ranges for books in your genre and look at books by other authors. Think about your target audience and what they may be willing to pay.

What are your sales goals? If you want to have a high volume of sales, then you may consider a cheaper price; but if you want to cover your costs of producing and marketing your book, then you may need to keep your price at a higher rate in order to ensure you don't run at a loss. You should also explore any royalty charges on your distribution platform, as lower pricing may involve a higher proportion of royalty payment charges.

Long books will involve more production costs. If your book is very long, think about whether it would be feasible to change it into a series of books where you could build a market for sales, and also realise greater profit.

Introductory offers may attract sales and reviews, which in turn may produce more sales. Monitor your feedback and adjust your pricing if feedback indicates it is not value for money.

If you are pricing your book for a different country, ensure you match the price not just to the exchange rate, but also to the pricing of similar books in that country.

Pricing a book is a delicate balance of costs, profits and sale volume, so take advantage of your publishing team's knowledge and experience in this area so that your 'price is right'.

"Loving wisdom and not hungering for knowledge is impossible.
Because knowledge feeds wisdom."

CHAPTER

7

LOOKING TO THE FUTURE

You will have realised by now that the publishing world is dynamic and one that embraces change. This chapter will list some of the existing trends that have emerged over the last few years, and also consider where the publishing market is heading.

Whereas in the past authors used their imagination to develop their stories and content, people involved in publishing can now consider many new and diverse ways to publish that content, get support, and ensure their work is protected.

The need for multi-format content, not just printed material, but e-Book and audio, is now well established. Going a step further and bringing massive change, is the ability to offer immersive experiences, where the story comes to life. AR/VR storytelling uses augmented reality or virtual reality to help readers engage with the story, identifying with characters, and even change the endings. It can present 'real life' experience of what is being written about, enhancing the ability to learn and remember the topic. Dynamic QR codes referred to in the previous chapter, can provide an entry portal to this world, and my expectation is that this element of publishing will continue to grow and develop very quickly.

As trad publishers are overtaken by the boom in self- and hybrid-publishing routes, there is a move by publishing companies to offer more variety in their publishing methods, for example coming alongside authors who want to self-publish by offering partnerships instead of the traditional contracts. This route offers less risk for the publisher, who can connect with a healthy 'author pool' and build relationships for future publishing opportunities. Hybrid publishers are also offering wider choice in the packages they offer, recognising that authors are often more engaged in preparing books for publication and are also becoming much more involved in marketing, so the packages they offer are more flexible.

AI is already offering a wealth of editing help, although it comes with a caution warning. It can help rephrase, bring a new tone, and even offer additional ideas to improve content. The apps listed in *Get Writing* help in this area, and this support can only develop and increase.

Print on demand has meant that estimating sales in advance is no longer an issue, and is more sustainable. Linked to this is the author/reader relationship, which is becoming more and more personal through targeted advertising, social media, indie publisher groups, and direct-to-consumer models.

Perhaps one of the most interesting emerging developments is in the field of Intellectual Property (IP) rights. In the past it has been quite difficult to manage copyright issues, but now the development of blockchain technology can track and verify ownership of digital content. It can also seamlessly manage contracts, distribution and licensing. This is an area that is still developing, but worth watching, as it has the potential to offer more connection between authors and readers, more flexibility, and a simpler way to manage sales.

"Every problem is an opportunity to become better, to know better and to do better."

CHAPTER
8

TO SUMMARISE

You're now well on the way to understanding the many elements that are involved in publishing your book, bringing it to print and becoming established as an author, and your new awareness should help you avoid the stumbling blocks that may occur in your print journey.

The pitfalls of the DIY approach are evident, and also the difficulties associated with the trad publishing route. A good hybrid publisher gives you flexibility, and also offers a reliable way to ensure that your book gets the best start in its journey out into the world.

Hold in mind the experiences of other published authors when they think back about getting their book in print. Some common regrets are that they allowed errors – grammatical and formatting – to remain in their manuscript. They then kick themselves as, of course, these errors were glaringly obvious as soon as they had published. Another common regret is that the blurb – information on the front and back covers – was rushed and was not as powerful in attracting new readers as it could have been. Cover design is another area where authors wished they had been more forceful in getting their designer to do a better job. And there are aspects of marketing that could have been better, and that is covered in detail in our book on marketing and promoting your book strategically in an international market. The point here is that you should take your time and ensure that everything is thoroughly checked before you have rushed to publish and print, and I write this from the experience of having sold thousands of my own books, and helping other authors do the same.

Vike Springs Publications are at hand to answer any questions you have, and to help you in your publishing journey, making sure you can get your published book to your audience. We understand the process from writing to publication, and we are uniquely placed to offer comprehensive packages that best suit your needs and avoid the stress and complications that are so often part of the publishing process. All you need to do is focus on your ideas and develop your vision. We can worry about the rest! Know that we can provide all that you need – from ghostwriting, editing, layout and design, formatting to proofreading, publishing, global distribution and marketing.

With over 115 years of cumulative experience in the publishing industry, spanning various disciplines, our team of experts have what it takes to make your authorship dream a great success. The services we offer are tailored to provide you with comprehensive packages that best serve your needs and take away the hassle and complications associated with the publishing process.

We also have a real presence in the international book publishing world, which is explained in detail in *Promote Your Book*. Vike Springs has a passion for assisting authors from around the world, with links into global marketing platforms. We produce world class quality books and can give our authors maximum exposure around the globe.

Reading about the areas of writing and marketing in this three-book series will add to your toolkit of knowledge. Don't hesitate to get in touch with us to find out more about how we can meet your specific requirements. A full list of our range of services is set out in Appendix 1.

APPENDIX 1
STANDARD BOOK PUBLISHING PROPOSAL

Dear Author,
Thank you very much for your interest in our services.

Vike Springs Publishing Ltd. is an international publishing house based in London, United Kingdom, and a proud member of **IBPA** (Independent Book Publishers Association) **USA**.

As a Publishing House we are driven by the vision to work with authors in publishing world-class quality books and giving them maximum exposure around the globe. We are confident that with our team of industry professionals we can work with you to help you share your work, expertise, and knowledge with the global community.

Our **Comprehensive Self-Publishing** packages, we believe, would be of great benefit to you. From comprehensive editorial and proofreading services, custom interior layout and cover design, standout author branding packages to effective marketing and promotion packages, these services have been put together to afford you the flexibility to choose the one that meets your unique needs. You will also enjoy the freedom of choosing the sale price and earn 100% of your royalties received from all major bookseller platforms worldwide.

COMPREHENSIVE SELF-PUBLISHING PACKAGES

Standard Packages	Silver	Gold	Platinum
ISBN Assignment & UPC Barcode	✓	✓	✓
Books in Print Registration	✓	✓	✓
Editorial Assessment	✓	✓	✓
Content Editing, Copyediting & Plagiarism Checks	✓	✓	✓
Proofreading	✓	✓	✓
Custom Book Interior Layout Design	✓	✓	✓
Custom Book Cover Design with 3D copies	✓	✓	✓
E-Book Formatting & Publishing	✓	✓	✓
Barnes & Noble "Read Instantly"	✓	✓	✓
One-on-One Support & S Media Marketing Advice	✓	✓	✓
Amazon "Look Inside" and Google Preview	✓	✓	✓
Worldwide Book Distribution	✓	✓	✓
Paperback and Hardback Publishing	✓	✓	✓
FREE Complimentary Author Paperback Copies *	TBC	TBC	TBC
Author Brand Promo (Electronic Flyer & Posters)	—	✓	✓
Social Media Intro Promo Launch	—	✓	✓
Audiobook Production & Publishing	—	—	✓
Marketing & Promotion	—	—	✓

Reach out to us for our two-page publishing proposal for your consideration.

We also offer ghostwriting services, and developmental writing services. Each of these options provide a great opportunity to get all your ideas and thoughts set out professionally, in a way that can have the maximum impact on your intended audience.

An added benefit of our services is helping you publish your book on all global book platforms, such as, **Amazon global, Barnes and Noble, Ingram, Kindle, Smashwords, Draft2Digital, Apple iBooks, Gardners & Extended Retailer, Odilo, WHSmith (Kobo), Scribd, Baker & Taylor, Tolino, OverDrive, Bibliotheca, Palace Marketplace, Vivlio, Borrowbox, Everand, Fable, Hoopla, public libraries,** with direct access to **Independent Bookstore buyers** in the **USA, North America** and **Europe**, and many more, in both eBook, paperback, hardback and audiobook formats, as well as providing world class quality book printing services, delivered on time to your chosen address.

Your book would also be made available on the global book inventory system, accessed by independent booksellers, libraries, and wholesale book buyers around the world.

We would love to hear from you on how we can work with you to make your work available to the wider global community. We hope you find your best fit package from our full range of packages for your consideration. If not, we would be more than glad to deliver a custom package that meets your requirements.

Hope to hear from you soon.
Thank you.

APPENDIX 2

AUTHOR REVIEWS

"My experience with Vike Springs Publishing Ltd has been a rewarding and exciting one indeed! They provided me with a friendly, proactive, conscientious, professional and value-for-money publishing service. ... I've already started referring their services to friends and colleagues in my network of contacts." **Kofi Ayeh,** Author of ***The Debt Trap: Understanding the Global Cost of Living Crisis. Luton - UK***

"...The Vike Springs team take on your project with professionalism and a personal passion to see you succeed. They offer great advice on how to market and help you post your book on all the relevant social media and platforms. ... I owe them my full gratitude as a first-time publisher." **Nii Kojo Addy,** Author of ***A Dangerous Journey To Stardom. London - UK***

"I would like to acknowledge Vike Springs Publishing for enabling my book ... to become a reality. Mr Victor ... virtually 'took over' the entire project. His daily communication, sincerity, patience and ingenuity all contributed to the book finally reaching fruition. With my second book in the pipeline I would look no further but to go back to Vike Springs. My personal thanks to Victor and his team for giving me peace of mind and fulfilling my dream." **Jenny Mohan,** Author of ***The King of Katunga. Accra - Ghana***

"... It's almost like 24-hour service. Their support encouraged and enabled me to successfully publish my first book. I will introduce them to others." **Max Ako,** Author of ***From Abraham: Journeys through the Bible covering the Old Testament, the Silent Period and the Ministry of Jesus till today. London - UK***

"I have enjoyed my experience with Vike Springs Publishing. They ... give a warm welcome to the world of literary publishing. ... patient, attentive to details and work with you on every step, making sure their delivery is on time. ... I am grateful to Vike Springs Publishing for their professional work ... in producing such an excellent book, and I would recommend their service ..." ***Lavern Powell,*** Author of ***Grace For Purpose And Thanksgiving". London - UK***

ENDNOTES

[1]   Kwegyir, V. Business *365: Daily Inspiration for Creativity, Innovation and Business Success.* Vike Springs Publishing Ltd (23 July 2020)

[2]   Rushdie, Salman. *Joseph Anton. A Memoir.* Vintage (2013)

[3]   Publish Drive. *How to Crowdfund your Book.* https://publishdrive.com/how-to-crowdfund-your-book.html

[4]   Blurb Blog. *Book Trends to Look for in 2024. https://www.blurb.com/blog/book-publishing-trends/*

[5]   GW & Co. *What you Need to Know About Writing and Publishing Trends in 2024.* https://ghostwritersandco.com/publishing-trends/

[6]   Future Market Insights Inc. *Book Publishers Market.* https://www.futuremarketinsights.com/reports/book-publishers-market

[7]   Alliance of Independent Authors https://annafeatherstone.com/allis-big-indie-author-data-drop-2024/ (Sourcing K-Lytics 2024)

[8]   Voices. *Audiobook Listening Trends.* https://www.voices.com/company/press/reports/audiobook-habits

[9]   GW & Co. *How Many Books Were Published Last Year? (2024 Statistics)* https://ghostwritersandco.com/books-published-last-year/

[10]   Future Management Insights Inc./Book Publishers Market. *Ibid.*

www.ingramcontent.com/pod-product-compliance
Lightning Source LLC
La Vergne TN
LVHW051816080426
835513LV00017B/1984